DiscoverRoo
An Imprint of Pop!
popbooksonline.com

The Eras of Taylor Swift

THE FOLKLORE era

Track List

1. the 1
2. cardigan
3. the last great american dynasty
4. exile (ft. Bon Iver)
5. my tears ricochet
6. mirrorball
7. seven
8. august
9. this is me trying
10. illicit affairs
11. invisible string
12. mad woman
13. epiphany
14. betty
15. peace
16. hoax

by Elizabeth Andrews

WELCOME TO DiscoverRoo!

This book is filled with videos, puzzles, games, and more! Scan the QR codes* while you read, or visit the website below to make this book pop.

popbooksonline.com/Folklore

abdobooks.com

Published by Pop!, a division of ABDO, PO Box 398166, Minneapolis, Minnesota 55439.

Printed in the United States of America, North Mankato, Minnesota.

082025
012026

Cover Photo: Alexandra Tarasova (BigArtLab); Shutterstock Images

Interior Photos: Getty Images; PaoloV/Flickr; Shutterstock Images; Stephen Chung/Alamy; WENN Rights Ltd/Alamy; Zoran Veselinovic/Retna/Avalon/Newscom; ZUMA Press, Inc./Alamy

Editors: Grace Hansen and Anna Schwartz

Series Designer: Laura Graphenteen

Library of Congress Control Number: 2025941222

Publisher's Cataloging-in-Publication Data

Names: Andrews, Elizabeth, author.

Title: The Folklore era / by Elizabeth Andrews

Description: Minneapolis, Minnesota : Pop!, 2026 | Series: The eras of Taylor Swift | Includes online resources and index

Identifiers: ISBN 9781098248703 (lib. bdg.) | ISBN 9781098249229 (ebook)

Subjects: LCSH: Swift, Taylor, 1989- --Juvenile literature. | Popular music--Juvenile literature. | Popular (Songs, etc.)--Juvenile literature. | Albums--Juvenile literature. | Concerts--Juvenile literature. | Mass media and music--Juvenile literature.

Classification: DDC 782.42164095--dc23

*Scanning QR codes requires a web-enabled smart device with a QR code reader app and a camera.

TABLE OF CONTENTS

CHAPTER 1
A Surprise to Everyone 4

CHAPTER 2
Discovering *Folklore* 12

CHAPTER 3
Telling Stories 18

CHAPTER 4
Folklore in the World 24

Making Connections. 30
Glossary 31
Index. 32
Online Resources 32

CHAPTER 1

A SURPRISE TO EVERYONE

On July 23, 2020, nine new photos took over Taylor Swift's Instagram grid. Individually, the photos were blurs of black and white and trees. Together, the photos formed an image of Taylor standing alone in a forest. She also posted a message to fans announcing her surprise eighth **studio** album, *folklore*.

WATCH A VIDEO HERE!

Meet Taylor

Birthday: December 13, 1989
Star Sign: Sagittarius
Place of Birth: West Reading, PA
Favorite Number: 13
Favorite Color: Purple
Favorite Food: Chicken tenders and a chocolate shake

Meredith Grey

13

Benjamin Button

XOXO

Olivia Benson

Taylor Swift

Taylor told fans there were a lot of Easter eggs in folklore. *These are secret messages and clues in Taylor's work.*

The summer of 2020 was a lonely time for people all over the world. They were in the middle of the global COVID-19 **pandemic**. Taylor, like most people, was **isolating** in her home. She'd canceled her tour for *Lover*. Sitting on her couch at home, her imagination ran wild. So, Taylor began writing an album.

Taylor got inspiration for folklore's *imagery from the movies she watched while staying home, such as* Pan's Labyrinth *and* Jane Eyre.

On the same day that Taylor announced *folklore*, she released it. There was no wait time for fans to get excited or imagine what songs could be on the album. All at once, 16 new tracks were in fans' ears and they were different from anything Taylor had done before. The album is a mix of pop and **folk**. It is quiet and **melancholy**, which encourages listeners to consider their feelings deeply.

Taylor wore a long plaid coat, cardigan, white and flannel dresses, and boots for the album photo shoot.

Aaron Dessner (center) plays in The National. Jack Antonoff (left) plays in Bleachers.

Taylor worked with **producers** Jack Antonoff and Aaron Dessner to create *folklore*. Both men are successful musicians themselves. All three wrote and recorded virtually. Taylor recorded her vocals in a makeshift studio at her Los Angeles home. The production took place in New York City and at Long Pond Studio in the Hudson Valley.

DID YOU KNOW?

Taylor called her home recording setup Kitty Committee Studio.

CHAPTER 2

DISCOVERING *FOLKLORE*

Tales of folklore are passed down and written about over long periods of time. They often mix truth with fantasy. Taylor told fans in a letter about the album that most of the stories throughout *folklore* are not her own.

EXPLORE LINKS HERE!

The *folklore* cabin makes appearances in music videos and on tour.

Easter Egg

Folklore was released July 24th. The numbers of the date add up to 13 which is Taylor's favorite number.

7+2+4=13

Taylor wrote some songs with her boyfriend at the time, Joe Alwyn. He wrote under the name William Bowery.

The process of writing *folklore* was different than anything Taylor had done before. She usually writes autobiographical songs. This means her songs are about herself and her experiences. The *folklore* album is not about her. Taylor waited until shortly before the release of the album to tell her **label** because she was nervous about how it would be received. But everyone at the label was thrilled!

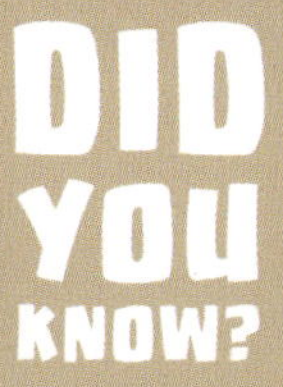

The fifth tracks on Taylor's albums are always her saddest. "My tears ricochet" is *folklore*'s track 5. It may be about Taylor's disagreement with her old label.

Taylor said she had images in her head when she began writing *folklore*. She imagined an old cardigan, a tree swing, hushed whispers of running away, and more.

A PARTNER IN "EXILE"

Taylor heard Joe Alwyn playing the piano as they were **isolating** at home. She wrote lyrics to go with his song. She told Dessner that it should be a duet. He agreed and suggested she sing it with his friend Justin Vernon. Vernon releases music as Bon Iver. Taylor has always been a big fan of his. When he agreed to sing on "exile," she couldn't believe it!

The images led her to create characters and then write their stories. Some of the characters are a man who lives all alone, an enemy who was once a friend, a seventeen-year-old learning to apologize, and Taylor's own grandfather, Dean.

The song "epiphany" is about Taylor's grandfather. It also mentions the devastation of the COVID-19 pandemic.

CHAPTER 3

TELLING STORIES

Taylor threads one particular story through the album. She calls it the teenage love triangle. She wrote three songs, each from a different perspective, about the same summer. She named the three characters James, Augustine, and Betty. One summer, James betrayed Betty by having a fling with Augustine.

COMPLETE AN ACTIVITY HERE!

A fling is short-lived romantic relationship.

The first song from the love triangle is "cardigan." This song is from Betty's perspective 20 to 30 years after the summer. She is reflecting on her and James' young love. This song was the first **single** from the album. The lines "to kiss in cars and downtown bars / was all we needed / you drew stars around my scars" are Easter eggs to two songs on *Lover.*

"August" is written from Augustine's point of view. This song shows that Augustine isn't a bad person who stole James away from Betty. She is **sensitive** and fell for James during a wonderful summer together. She shares how much she felt for him even though he was never truly hers. When James left after the summer was over, Augustine was heartbroken.

In Taylor's mind, Betty and James have a happily-ever-after.

"Betty" was another single from the album. It's a happy tune that sounds similar to early Taylor music. "Betty" lets fans finally hear James' side of the love triangle. It is about him learning to apologize for his mistakes. James comes home from his summer with Augustine and wants to get Betty back. He missed her. Taylor wrote this song with Joe.

The story in "the last great american dynasty" is about a real-life **socialite**,

Easter Egg

Betty and James are named after the children of Taylor's friends Blake Lively and Ryan Reynolds.

Jack Antonoff says "the last great american dynasty" is all about Taylor, even though it seems to be about someone else.

Rebekah Harkness. She lived in the house in Rhode Island that Taylor bought in 2013. Taylor always wanted to write a song about her but never felt like there was a track big enough for her story. Like Taylor, Harkness often lived her life in a way that some people found odd and dramatic.

CHAPTER 4

FOLKLORE IN THE WORLD

Taylor and her **producers** met up at Long Pond **Studio** to perform the album together for the first time. They hadn't had the chance before because of COVID-19 rules. While they played, they filmed the Long Pond Studio Sessions.

LEARN MORE HERE!

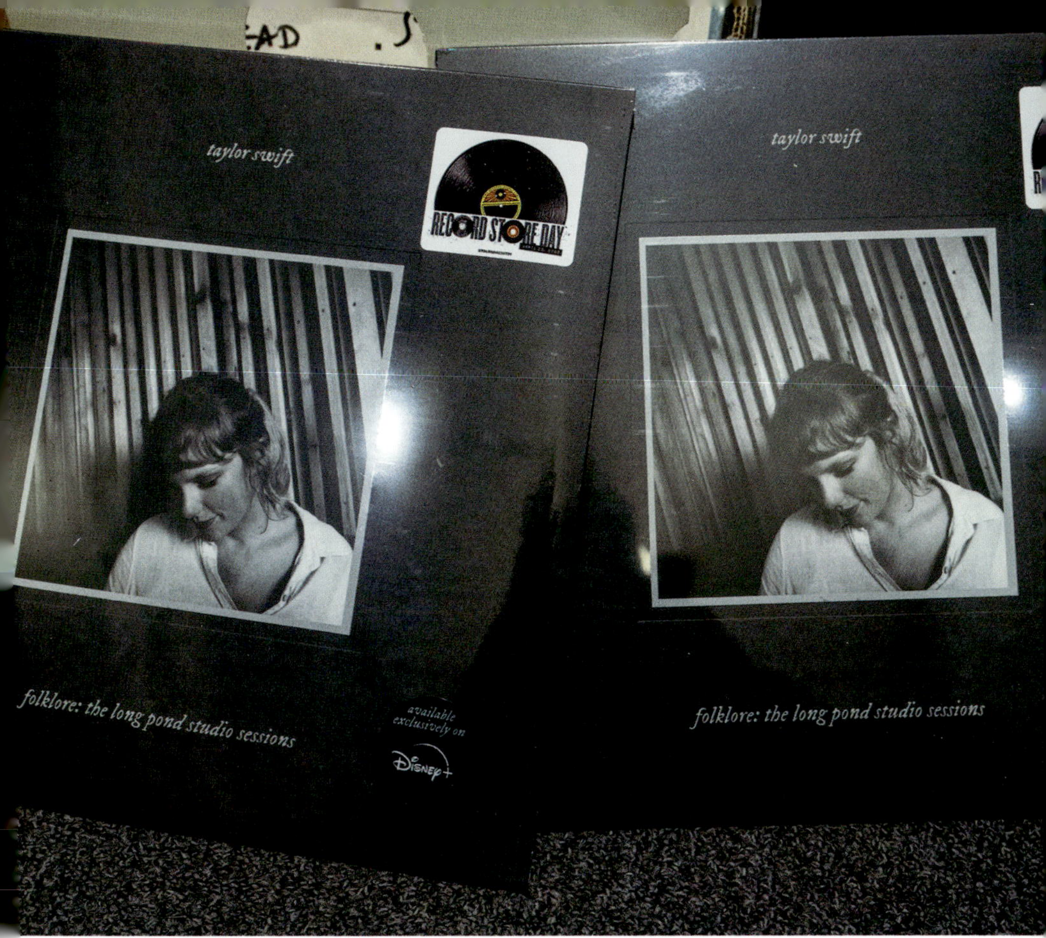

The Long Pond Studio Sessions were released as their own live album.

Before each song is performed, they discuss its meaning and recording process. A film of the calm and woodsy session was released on Disney+.

Taylor sang "the 1" on the roof of the folklore cabin. She was strapped in for safety.

Folklore had its own set on the Eras Tour until May 9, 2024, when Taylor combined it with *evermore*. The *folklore* set had a forest backdrop and moss-covered cabin. Taylor first introduced the cabin during her 2021 Grammy Awards performance. For *folklore*'s Eras set Taylor sang "the 1," "betty," "the last great american dynasty," "august," "illicit affairs," "my tears ricochet," and "cardigan."

At the start of the Eras Tour, Taylor opened the *folklore* set with "invisible string." After she broke up with Joe, she switched the opening song to "the 1."

Folklore was Taylor's third album to win the Grammy for Album of the Year. This made Taylor Swift the first woman to win the award three times. It has gone down in history as one of the best albums of all time according to the magazine *Rolling Stone* and Taylor Swift fans alike.

Taylor wore five different* folklore *dresses throughout the Eras Tour.

The Grammy Awards is an event that recognizes and awards remarkable works in music throughout the year.

MAKING CONNECTIONS

TEXT-TO-SELF

What is your favorite song from the *Folklore* Era? Why is it your favorite?

TEXT-TO-TEXT

Have you read books about any other music artists? How are they similar to or different from Taylor Swift?

TEXT-TO-WORLD

As a reader, why do you think so many people around the world connect with Taylor Swift and her music? Write a few sentences to explain your answer.

GLOSSARY

folk — a type of popular music based on traditional music that does not use electric instruments.

isolate — to stay apart from others.

label — a company that helps make and release music recordings.

melancholy — causing feelings of sadness.

pandemic — an outbreak of a disease that spreads across a large area.

producer — someone who organizes the creation of music recordings. The act or process of producing is production.

sensitive — feeling or noticing things quite sharply.

single — a song that is released as a stand-alone from the album.

socialite — a well-known person in a community.

studio — a place where recordings are made.

INDEX

Alwyn, Joe, 16, 22
Antonoff, Jack, 11
"august," 21, 27
Augustine, 18, 21–22
awards, 27–28

"betty," 22, 27
Betty, 18, 20–22

"cardigan," 20, 27
COVID-19, 7, 24

Dessner, Aaron, 11

Eras Tour, 27
evermore, 27
"exile," 16

folklore, 4, 8, 11–12, 15–16, 27–28

Harkness, Rebekah, 23

James, 18, 20–22

Long Pond Studio, 11, 24
Lover, 7, 20

"the last great american dynasty," 22, 27

writing, 7, 15–18, 21, 23

DiscoverRoo!
ONLINE RESOURCES

This book is filled with videos, puzzles, games, and more! Scan the QR codes* while you read, or visit the website below to make this book pop.

popbooksonline.com/Folklore

*Scanning QR codes requires a web-enabled smart device with a QR code reader app and a camera.